The Essential Diabetic Cookbook

Healthy and Tasty Recipes to Prevent and Control Diabetes to Help You Balance Your Blood Sugars

Kimberly Crooks

Table of Contents

The information in the following pages is broadly considered a truthful and accurate account of facts and as such, any inattention, use, or misuse of the information in question by the reader will render any resulting actions solely under their purview. There are no scenarios in which the publisher or the original author of this work can be in any fashion deemed liable for any hardship or damages that may befall them after undertaking information described herein.

Additionally, the information in the following pages is intended only for informational purposes and should thus be thought of as universal. As befitting its nature, it is presented without assurance regarding its prolonged validity or interim quality. Trademarks that are mentioned are done without written consent and can in no way be considered an endorsement from the trademark holder.

Introduction

Diabetes mellitus, commonly known just as diabetes, is a disease that affects our metabolism. The predominant characteristic of diabetes is an inability to create or utilize insulin, a hormone that moves sugar from our blood cells into the rest of our bodies' cells. This is crucial for us because we rely on that blood sugar to power our body and provide energy. High blood sugar, if left untreated, can lead to serious damage of our eyes, nerves, kidneys, and other major organs. There are two major types of diabetes, type 1 and type 2, with the latter being the most common of the two with over 90 percent of diabetics suffering from it (Centers for Disease Control and Prevention, 2019).

HOW DOES INSULIN WORK?

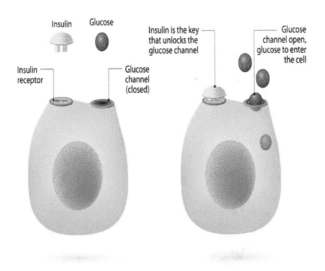

Insulin

Glucose

Insulin receptor

Glucose channel (closed)

Insulin is the key that unlocks the glucose channel

Glucose channel open, glucose to enter the cell

Type 1 diabetes is an autoimmune disease. In cases of type 1 diabetes, the immune system attacks cells in the pancreas responsible for insulin production. Although we are unsure what causes this reaction, many experts believe it is brought upon by a gene deficiency or by viral infections that may trigger the disease.

Type 1 Diabetes

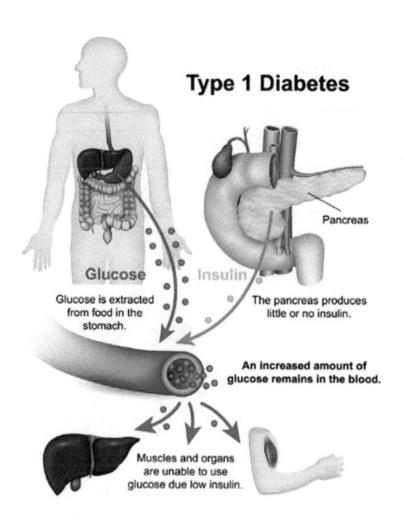

Pancreas

Glucose

Insulin

Glucose is extracted from food in the stomach.

The pancreas produces little or no insulin.

An increased amount of glucose remains in the blood.

Muscles and organs are unable to use glucose due low insulin.

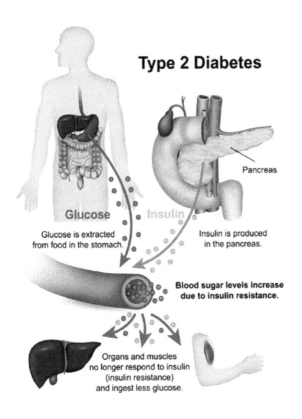

Type 2 Diabetes

Pancreas

Glucose

Insulin

Glucose is extracted
from food in the stomach.

Insulin is produced
in the pancreas.

**Blood sugar levels increase
due to insulin resistance.**

Organs and muscles
no longer respond to insulin
(insulin resistance)
and ingest less glucose.

Type 2 diabetes is a metabolic disorder, although research suggests it may warrant reclassification as an autoimmune disease as well. People who suffer from type 2 diabetes have a high resistance to insulin or an inability to produce enough insulin. Experts believe that type 2 diabetes is a result of a genetic predisposition in many people, which is further aggravated by obesity and other environmental triggers.

Diagnosis

Diabetes diagnosis has come incredibly far in the last few decades. Currently, there are two primary tests for diagnosing diabetes: the fasting plasma glucose (FPG) test and the hemoglobin A1c test.

The FPG test measures your blood sugar levels after an eight-hour fasting period; this helps to show if your body is processing glucose at a healthy rate.

The A1c test shows your blood sugar levels over the last three months. It does this by testing the amount of glucose being carried by the hemoglobin of your red blood cells. Hemoglobin has a lifespan of roughly three months; this allows us to test them to see how long they have been carrying their glucose for and how much they have.

Symptoms

In type 1 diabetes, the list of symptoms can be extensive with both serious and less obvious indicators. Below, I will list the most common symptoms as well as other potential complications of type 1 diabetes:

- **Excessive thirst:** Excessive thirst is one of the less noticeable indicators of type 1 diabetes. It is brought upon by high blood sugar (hyperglycemia).

- **Frequent urination:** Frequent urination is caused by your kidneys failing to process all of the glucose in your blood; this forces your body to attempt to flush out excess glucose through urinating.

- **Fatigue:** Fatigue in type 1 diabetes patients is caused by the body's inability to process glucose for energy.

- **Excessive hunger:** Those suffering from type 1 diabetes often have persistent hunger and increased appetites. This is because the body is desperate for glucose despite its inability to process it without insulin.

- **Cloudy or unclear vision:** Rapid fluctuations in blood sugar levels can lead to cloudy or blurred vision. Those suffering from untreated type 1 diabetes are unable to naturally control their blood sugar levels, making rapid fluctuations a very common occurrence.

- **Rapid weight loss:** Rapid weight loss is probably the most noticeable symptom of type 1 diabetes. As your body starves off glucose, it resorts to breaking down muscle and fat to sustain itself. This can lead to incredibly fast weight loss in type 1 diabetes cases.

SYMPTOMS OF TYPE 1 DIABETES

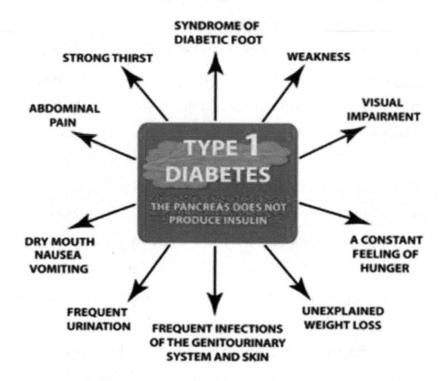

- **Ketoacidosis:** Ketoacidosis is a potentially deadly complication of untreated type 1 diabetes. In response to the lack of glucose being fed into your muscles and organs, your body starts breaking down your fat and muscle into an energy source called ketones, which can be burned without the need of insulin. Ketones are usually perfectly fine in normal amounts. But, when your body is starving, it may end up flooding itself with ketones in an attempt to fuel itself; the acidification of your blood that follows this influx of acid molecules may lead to more serious conditions, a coma, or death.

In cases of type 2 diabetes, the symptoms tend to be slower to develop, and they tend to be mild early on. Some early symptoms mimic type 1 diabetes and may include:

- **Excessive hunger:** Similar to type 1 diabetes, those of us with type 2 diabetes will feel constant hunger. Again, this is brought on by our bodies looking for fuel because of our inability to process glucose.

- **Fatigue and mental fog:** Depending on the severity of the insulin shortage in type 2 sufferers, they may feel physical fatigue and a mental fogginess during their average day.

- **Frequent urination:** Another symptom of both type 1 and 2 diabetes. Frequent urination is simply your body's way of attempting to rid itself of excess glucose.

- **Dry mouth and constant thirst:** It are unclear what causes dry mouth in diabetic sufferers, but it is tightly linked to high blood sugar levels. Constant thirst is brought on not only by a dry mouth but also by the dehydration that frequent urination causes.

SYMPTOMS OF TYPE 2 DIABETES

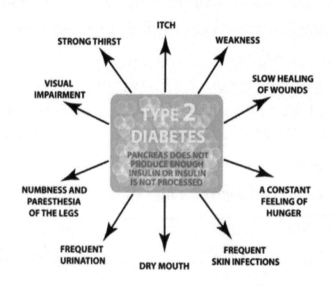

- **Itchy skin:** Itching of the skin, especially around the hands and feet, is a sign of polyneuropathy (diabetic nerve damage). As well as being a sign of potential nerve damage, itching can be a sign of high concentrations of cytokines circulating in your bloodstream; these are inflammatory molecules that can lead to itching. Cytokines are signaling proteins and hormonal regulators that are often released in high amounts before nerve damage.

As type 2 diabetes progresses and becomes more serious, the symptoms can become highly uncomfortable and dangerous. Some of these advanced symptoms include:

- **Slow healing of bruises, cuts, and abrasions:** Many people suffering from type 2 diabetes have impaired immune systems due to the lack of energy available to the body. As well as a lack of energy, many diabetics have slowed circulation brought upon by high blood glucose levels. Both of these factors lead to a much slower healing process and far greater risks of infection.

- **Yeast infections:** In women with type 2 diabetes, the chances of yeast infections are far higher than in non-diabetic women. This is due to high blood sugar levels and a lowered immune system response.

- **Neuropathy or numbness:** Long-term high blood sugar levels can lead to severe nerve damage in adults with diabetes. It is believed around 70 percent of people with type 2 diabetes have some form of neuropathy (Hoskins, 2020). Diabetic neuropathy is characterized by a numbness in the extremities, specifically around the feet and fingers.

- **Dark skin patches (acanthosis nigricans):** Some people with type 2 diabetes may have far above normal levels of insulin in their blood, as their body is unable to utilize it due to insulin resistance. This increase of insulin in the bloodstream can lead to some skin cells over reproducing and cause dark patches to form on the skin.

Complications

Severe complications of diabetes can be debilitating and deadly. Both type 1 and type 2 diabetes can lead to serious neurological, cardiovascular, and optical conditions. Some of the most common complications of advanced diabetes are as follows:

- **Heart attacks:** Diabetes is directly linked to a higher rate of heart attacks in adults. High blood glucose levels damage the cells and nerves around the heart and blood vessels over time, which can cause a plethora of heart diseases to form.

- **Cataracts:** People with diabetes have a nearly 60 percent greater chance of developing cataracts later in life if their diabetes is left unchecked (Diabetes.co.uk, 2019a). Doctors are unsure of the exact reason for cataracts forming at a higher rate in diabetes patients, but many believe it has to do with the lower amounts of glucose available to the cells powering our eyes.

- **Peripheral artery disease (PAD):** This is a very common diabetes and This causes decreased blood flow, which leads to serious issues in the lower legs, often resulting in amputation.

- **Diabetic nephropathy:** Diabetic nephropathy happens when high levels of blood glucose damage parts of your kidneys, which is responsible for filtering blood. This causes your kidneys to develop chronic kidney diseases and break down over time, leading to failure.

- **Glaucoma:** Diabetes can cause glaucoma in sufferers due to high blood sugar levels and this directly damages blood vessels in the eyes. When your body attempts to repair these vessels, it may cause glaucoma on the iris where the damage was caused.

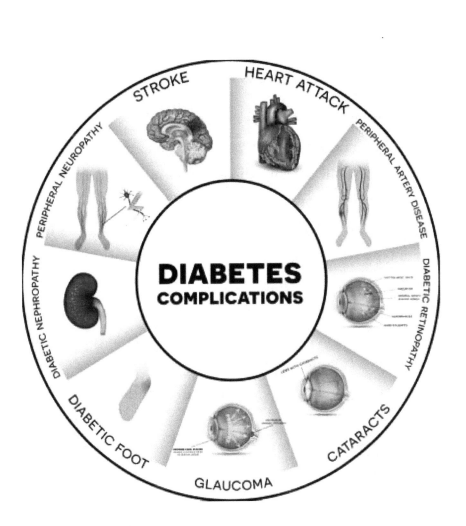

Treatment

Treatments for diabetes vary depending on the type, number, and severity of complications and health of the patient overall. Luckily, diabetes has been long studied by the medical community and, therefore, there is an abundance of resources and treatments available.

For type 1 diabetes, insulin supplements are essential. Type 1 diabetics rely on daily insulin injections; some prefer a costlier but easier-to-use insulin pump. Insulin needs in type 1 diabetics will vary throughout the day as they eat and exercise. This means many type 1 diabetics will regularly test their blood sugar levels to assess whether their insulin needs are being met.

Some type 1 diabetics develop insulin resistance after years of injections. This means that oral diabetes medication such as metformin is becoming increasingly more commonly prescribed to type 1 diabetics to help prevent insulin resistance.

Type 2 diabetes can be controlled without medication in some cases. Many type 2 diabetics can self-regulate their blood sugar levels through careful eating and light exercise. Most type 2 diabetics are recommended to stay on low-fat diets, which are high in fiber and healthy carbs.

Some type 2 diabetics do need medication. Unlike type 1, insulin is not nearly as commonly needed for type 2. But, some type 2 diabetics do need insulin to supplement the reduced amount their pancreas may provide.

The most common medication given to type 2 diabetics is metformin. This prescription drug helps lower blood glucose levels and improve insulin sensitivity. Other drugs prescribed to type 2 diabetics include sulfonylureas, thiazolidinediones, and meglitinides, which all help increase insulin production or sensitivity.

Diabetes
Blood Sugar Level

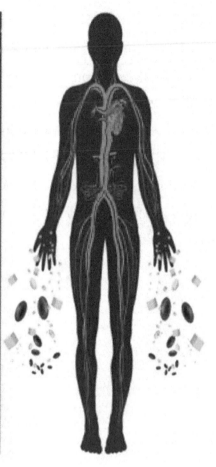

HBA-1C Test Score	Mean Blood mg/dl	Glucose mmol/l
14.0	380	21.1
13.0	350	19.3
12.0	315	17.4
11.0	280	15.6
10.0	250	13.7
9.0	215	11.9
8.0	180	10.0
7.0	150	8.2
6.0	115	6.3
5.0	80	4.7
4.0	50	2.6
3.0	35	2.0

Action Suggested

Good

Excellent

- Very high
- A little high to very high depending on patient
- Maximum after meal in nondiabetics
- Normal before meal in nondiabetics
- Normal
- Low
- Extremely low

" The normal range of blood sugar according to the glucose levels chart is between 70 and 100 mg/dl "

10 Tips to Control Diabetes

- **Eat less salt:** Salt can increase your chances of having high blood pressure, which leads to increased chances of heart disease and stroke.

- **Replace sugar:** Replace sugar with zero calorie sweeteners. Cutting out sugar gives you much more control over your blood sugar levels.

- **Cut out alcohol:** Alcohol tends to be high in calories, and if drunk on an empty stomach with insulin medication, it can cause drastic drops in blood sugar.

- **Be physically active:** Physical activity lowers your risk of cardiovascular issues and increases your body's natural glucose burn rate.

- **Avoid saturated fats:** Saturated fats like butter and pastries can lead to high cholesterol and blood circulation issues.

- **Use canola or olive oil:** If you need to use oil in your cooking, use canola or olive oil. Both are high in beneficial fatty acids and monounsaturated fat.

- **Drink water:** Water is by far the healthiest drink you can have. Drinking water helps to regulate blood sugar and insulin levels.

- **Make sure you get enough vitamin D:** Vitamin D is a crucial vitamin for controlling blood sugar levels. Eat food high in this vitamin or ask your doctor about supplements.
- **Avoid processed food:** Processed foods tend to be high in vegetable oils, salt, refined grains, or other unhealthy additives.
- **Drink coffee and tea:** Not only are coffee and tea great hunger suppressants for dieters, but they contain important antioxidants that help with protecting cells.

Chipotle Chili Pork Chops

Preparation Time: 4 hours

Cooking Time: 20 minutes

Serving: 4

Ingredients:

- Juice and zest of 1 lime
- 1 tablespoon extra-virgin olive oil
- 1 tablespoon chipotle chili powder
- 2 teaspoons minced garlic
- 1 teaspoon ground cinnamon
- Pinch sea salt
- 4 (5-ounce) pork chops

Direction:

1. Combine the lime juice and zest, oil, chipotle chili powder, garlic, cinnamon, and salt in a resealable plastic bag. Add the pork chops. Remove as much air as possible and seal the bag.

2. Marinate the chops in the refrigerator for at least 4 hours, and up to 24 hours, turning them several times.

3. Ready the oven to 400°F and set a rack on a baking sheet. Let the chops rest at room temperature for 15 minutes, then arrange them on the rack and discard the remaining marinade.

4. Roast the chops until cooked through, turning once, about 10 minutes per side.

5. Serve with lime wedges.

Nutrition:
204 Calories
1g Carbohydrates
1g Sugar

Orange-Marinated Pork Tenderloin

Preparation Time: 2 hours

Cooking Time: 30 minutes

Serving: 4

Ingredients:

- ¼ cup freshly squeezed orange juice

- 2 teaspoons orange zest

- 2 teaspoons minced garlic

- 1 teaspoon low-sodium soy sauce

- 1 teaspoon grated fresh ginger

- 1 teaspoon honey

- 1½ pounds pork tenderloin roast

- 1 tablespoon extra-virgin olive oil

Direction:

1. Blend together the orange juice, zest, garlic, soy sauce, ginger, and honey.

2. Pour the marinade into a resealable plastic bag and add the pork tenderloin.

3. Remove as much air as possible and seal the bag. Marinate the pork in the refrigerator, turning the bag a few times, for 2 hours.

4. Preheat the oven to 400°F.

5. Pull out tenderloin from the marinade and discard the marinade.

6. Position big ovenproof skillet over medium-high heat and add the oil.

7. Sear the pork tenderloin on all sides, about 5 minutes in total.

8. Position skillet to the oven and roast for 25 minutes.

9. Put aside for 10 minutes before serving.

Nutrition:
228 Calories
4g Carbohydrates
3g Sugar

Homestyle Herb Meatballs

Preparation Time: 10 minutes

Cooking Time: 15 minutes

Serving: 4

Ingredients:

- ½ pound lean ground pork

- ½ pound lean ground beef

- 1 sweet onion, finely chopped

- ¼ cup bread crumbs

- 2 tablespoons chopped fresh basil

- 2 teaspoons minced garlic

- 1 egg

Direction:

1. Preheat the oven to 350°F.

2. Ready baking tray with parchment paper and set it aside.

3. In a large bowl, mix together the pork, beef, onion, bread crumbs, basil, garlic, egg, salt, and pepper until very well mixed.

4. Roll the meat mixture into 2-inch meatballs.

5. Transfer the meatballs to the baking sheet and bake until they are browned and cooked through, about 15 minutes.

6. Serve the meatballs with your favorite marinara sauce and some steamed green beans.

Nutrition:

332 Calories

13g Carbohydrates

3g Sugar

Lime-Parsley Lamb Cutlets

Preparation Time: 4 hours

Cooking Time: 10 minutes

Serving: 4

Ingredients:

- ¼ cup extra-virgin olive oil

- ¼ cup freshly squeezed lime juice

- 2 tablespoons lime zest

- 2 tablespoons chopped fresh parsley

- 12 lamb cutlets (about 1½ pounds total)

Direction:

1. Scourge the oil, lime juice, zest, parsley, salt, and pepper.

2. Pour marinade to a resealable plastic bag.

3. Add the cutlets to the bag and remove as much air as possible before sealing.

4. Marinate the lamb in the refrigerator for about 4 hours, turning the bag several times.

5. Preheat the oven to broil.

6. Remove the chops from the bag and arrange them on an aluminum foil–lined baking sheet. Discard the marinade.

7. Broil the chops for 4 minutes per side for medium doneness.

8. Let the chops rest for 5 minutes before serving.

Nutrition:

413 Calories

1g Carbohydrates

31g Protein

Mediterranean Steak Sandwiches

Preparation Time: 1 hour

Cooking Time: 10 minutes

Serving: 4

Ingredients:

- 2 tablespoons extra-virgin olive oil

- 2 tablespoons balsamic vinegar

- 2 teaspoons garlic

- 2 teaspoons lemon juice

- 2 teaspoons fresh oregano

- 1 teaspoon fresh parsley

- 1-pound flank steak

- 4 whole-wheat pitas

- 2 cups shredded lettuce

- 1 red onion, thinly sliced

- 1 tomato, chopped

- 1 ounce low-sodium feta cheese

Direction:

1. Scourge olive oil, balsamic vinegar, garlic, lemon juice, oregano, and parsley.

2. Add the steak to the bowl, turning to coat it completely.

3. Marinate the steak for 1 hour in the refrigerator, turning it over several times.

4. Preheat the broiler. Line a baking sheet with aluminum foil.

5. Put steak out of the bowl and discard the marinade.

6. Situate steak on the baking sheet and broil for 5 minutes per side for medium.

7. Set aside for 10 minutes before slicing.

8. Stuff the pitas with the sliced steak, lettuce, onion, tomato, and feta.

Nutrition:
344 Calories
22g Carbohydrates
3g Fiber

Roasted Beef with Peppercorn Sauce

Preparation Time: 10 minutes

Cooking Time: 90 minutes

Serving: 4

Ingredients:

- 1½ pounds top rump beef roast

- 3 teaspoons extra-virgin olive oil

- 3 shallots, minced

- 2 teaspoons minced garlic

- 1 tablespoon green peppercorns

- 2 tablespoons dry sherry

- 2 tablespoons all-purpose flour

- 1 cup sodium-free beef broth

Direction:

1. Heat the oven to 300°F.

2. Season the roast with salt and pepper.

3. Position huge skillet over medium-high heat and add 2 teaspoons of olive oil.

4. Brown the beef on all sides, about 10 minutes in total, and transfer the roast to a baking dish.

5. Roast until desired doneness, about 1½ hours for medium. When the roast has been in the oven for 1 hour, start the sauce.

6. In a medium saucepan over medium-high heat, sauté the shallots in the remaining 1 teaspoon of olive oil until translucent, about 4 minutes.

7. Stir in the garlic and peppercorns, and cook for another minute. Whisk in the sherry to deglaze the pan.

8. Whisk in the flour to form a thick paste, cooking for 1 minute and stirring constantly.

9. Fill in the beef broth and whisk for 4 minutes. Season the sauce.

10. Serve the beef with a generous spoonful of sauce.

Nutrition:
330 Calories
4g Carbohydrates
36g Protein

Coffee-and-Herb-Marinated Steak

Preparation Time: 2 hours

Cooking Time: 10 minutes

Serving: 3

Ingredients:

- ¼ cup whole coffee beans

- 2 teaspoons garlic

- 2 teaspoons rosemary

- 2 teaspoons thyme

- 1 teaspoon black pepper

- 2 tablespoons apple cider vinegar

- 2 tablespoons extra-virgin olive oil

- 1-pound flank steak, trimmed of visible fat

Direction:

1. Place the coffee beans, garlic, rosemary, thyme, and black pepper in a coffee grinder or food processor and pulse until coarsely ground.

2. Transfer the coffee mixture to a resealable plastic bag and add the vinegar and oil. Shake to combine.

3. Add the flank steak and squeeze the excess air out of the bag. Seal it. Marinate the steak in the refrigerator for at least 2 hours, occasionally turning the bag over.

4. Preheat the broiler. Line a baking sheet with aluminum foil.

5. Pull the steak out and discard the marinade.

6. Position steak on the baking sheet and broil until it is done to your liking.

7. Put aside for 10 minutes before cutting it.

8. Serve with your favorite side dish.

Nutrition:
313 Calories
20g Fat
31g Protein

Traditional Beef Stroganoff

Preparation Time: 10 minutes

Cooking Time: 30 minutes

Serving: 4

Ingredients:

- 1 teaspoon extra-virgin olive oil

- 1-pound top sirloin, cut into thin strips

- 1 cup sliced button mushrooms

- ½ sweet onion, finely chopped

- 1 teaspoon minced garlic

- 1 tablespoon whole-wheat flour

- ½ cup low-sodium beef broth

- ¼ cup dry sherry

- ½ cup fat-free sour cream

- 1 tablespoon chopped fresh parsley

Direction:

1. Position the skillet over medium-high heat and add the oil.

2. Sauté the beef until browned, about 10 minutes, then remove the beef with a slotted spoon to a plate and set it aside.

3. Add the mushrooms, onion, and garlic to the skillet and sauté until lightly browned, about 5 minutes.

4. Whisk in the flour and then whisk in the beef broth and sherry.

5. Return the sirloin to the skillet and bring the mixture to a boil.

6. Reduce the heat to low and simmer until the beef is tender, about 10 minutes.

7. Stir in the sour cream and parsley. Season with salt and pepper.

Nutrition:
257 Calories
6g Carbohydrates
1g Fiber

Chicken and Roasted Vegetable Wraps

Preparation Time: 10 minutes

Cooking Time: 20 minutes

Serving: 4

Ingredients:

- ½ small eggplant

- 1 red bell pepper

- 1 medium zucchini

- ½ small red onion, sliced

- 1 tablespoon extra-virgin olive oil

- 2 (8-ounce) cooked chicken breasts, sliced

- 4 whole-wheat tortilla wraps

Direction:

1. Preheat the oven to 400°F.

2. Wrap baking sheet with foil and set it aside.

3. In a large bowl, toss the eggplant, bell pepper, zucchini, and red onion with the olive oil.

4. Transfer the vegetables to the baking sheet and lightly season with salt and pepper.

5. Roast the vegetables until soft and slightly charred, about 20 minutes.

6. Divide the vegetables and chicken into four portions.

7. Wrap 1 tortilla around each portion of chicken and grilled vegetables, and serve.

Nutrition:
483 Calories
45g Carbohydrates
3g Fiber

Spicy Chicken Cacciatore

Preparation Time: 20 minutes

Cooking Time: 1 hour

Serving: 6

Ingredients:

- 1 (2-pound) chicken

- ¼ cup all-purpose flour

- 2 tablespoons extra-virgin olive oil

- 3 slices bacon

- 1 sweet onion

- 2 teaspoons minced garlic

- 4 ounces button mushrooms, halved

- 1 (28-ounce) can low-sodium stewed tomatoes

- ½ cup red wine

- 2 teaspoons chopped fresh oregano

Direction:

1. Cut the chicken into pieces: 2 drumsticks, 2 thighs, 2 wings, and 4 breast pieces.

2. Dredge the chicken pieces in the flour and season each piece with salt and pepper.

3. Place a large skillet over medium-high heat and add the olive oil.

4. Brown the chicken pieces on all sides, about 20 minutes in total. Transfer the chicken to a plate.

5. Cook chopped bacon to the skillet for 5 minutes. With a slotted spoon, transfer the cooked bacon to the same plate as the chicken.

6. Pour off most of the oil from the skillet, leaving just a light coating. Sauté the onion, garlic, and mushrooms in the skillet until tender, about 4 minutes.

7. Stir in the tomatoes, wine, oregano, and red pepper flakes.

8. Bring the sauce to a boil. Return the chicken and bacon, plus any accumulated juices from the plate, to the skillet.

9. Reduce the heat to low and simmer until the chicken is tender, about 30 minutes.

Nutrition:
230 Calories
14g Carbohydrates
2g Fiber

Salad

Thai Quinoa Salad

Preparation time: 10 minutes

Cooking time: 0 minutes

Servings: 1-2

Ingredients:
Ingredients used for dressing:

- 1 tbsp. Sesame seed

- 1 tsp. Chopped garlic

- 1 tsp. Lemon, fresh juice

- 3 tsp. Apple Cider Vinegar

- 2 tsp. Tamari, gluten-free.

- 1/4 cup of tahini (sesame butter)

- 1 pitted date

- 1/2 tsp. Salt

- 1/2 tsp. toasted Sesame oil

Salad Ingredients:

- 1 cup of quinoa, steamed

- 1 big handful of arugula

- 1 tomato cut in pieces

- 1/4 of the red onion, diced

Directions:

1. Add the following to a small blender: 1/4 cup + 2 tbsp.

2. Filtered water, the rest of the **Ingredients**. Blend, man. Steam 1 cup of quinoa in a steamer or a rice pan, then set aside.

3. Combine the quinoa, the arugula, the tomatoes sliced, the red onion diced on a serving plate or bowl, add the Thai dressing

4. and serve with a spoon.

Nutrition:

Calories: 100

Carbohydrates: 12 g

Green Goddess Bowl and Avocado Cumin Dressing

Preparation time: 10 minutes

Cooking time: 0 minutes

Servings: 1-2

Ingredients:

Ingredients for the dressing of avocado cumin:

- 1 Avocado

- 1 tbsp. Cumin Powder

- 2 limes, freshly squeezed

- 1 cup of filtered water

- 1/4 seconds. sea salt

- 1 tbsp. Olive extra virgin olive oil

- Cayenne pepper dash

- Optional: 1/4 tsp. Smoked pepper

Tahini Lemon Dressing Ingredients:

- 1/4 cup of tahini (sesame butter)

- 1/2 cup of filtered water (more if you want thinner, less thick)

- 1/2 lemon, freshly squeezed

- 1 clove of minced garlic

- 3/4 tsp. Sea salt (Celtic Gray, Himalayan, Redmond Real Salt)

- 1 tbsp. Olive extra virgin olive oil

- black pepper taste

Salad Ingredients:

- 3 cups of kale, chopped

- 1/2 cup of broccoli flowers, chopped

- 1/2 zucchini (make spiral noodles)

- 1/2 cup of kelp noodles, soaked and drained

- 1/3 cup of cherry tomatoes, halved.

- 2 tsp. hemp seeds

Directions:

1. Gently steam the kale and the broccoli (flash the steam for 4 minutes), set aside.

2. Mix the zucchini noodles and kelp noodles and toss with a generous portion of the smoked avocado cumin dressing. Add the cherry tomatoes and stir again.

3. Place the steamed kale and broccoli and drizzle with the lemon tahini dressing. Top the kale and the broccoli with the noodles and tomatoes and sprinkle the whole dish with the hemp seeds.

Nutrition:

Calories: 89

Carbohydrates: 11g

Fat: 1.2g

Protein: 4g

7 Sweet and Savory Salad

Preparation time: 10 minutes

Cooking time: 0 minutes

Servings: 1-2

Ingredients:

- 1 big head of butter lettuce

- 1/2 of cucumber, sliced

- 1 pomegranate, seed or 1/3 cup of seed

- 1 avocado, 1 cubed

- 1/4 cup of shelled pistachio, chopped

Ingredients for dressing:

- 1/4 cup of apple cider vinegar

- 1/2 cup of olive oil

- 1 clove of garlic, minced

Directions:

1. Put the butter lettuce in a salad bowl.

2. Add the remaining **Ingredients** and toss with the salad dressing.

Nutrition:

Calories: 68

Carbohydrates: 8g

Fat: 1.2g

Protein: 2g

Kale Pesto's Pasta

Preparation time: 10 minutes

Cooking time: 0 minutes

Servings: 1-2

Ingredients:

- 1 bunch of kale

- 2 cups of fresh basil

- 1/4 cup of extra virgin olive oil

- 1/2 cup of walnuts

- 2 limes, freshly squeezed

- Sea salt and chili pepper

- 1 zucchini, noodle (spiralizer)

- Optional: garnish with chopped asparagus, spinach leaves, and tomato.

Directions:

1. The night before, soak the walnuts in order to improve absorption.

2. Put all the recipe **Ingredients** in a blender and blend until the consistency of the cream is reached.

3. Add the zucchini noodles and enjoy.

Nutrition:

Calories: 55

Carbohydrates: 9 g

Fat: 1.2g

Beet Salad with Basil Dressing

Preparation time: 10 minutes

Cooking time: 0 minutes

Servings: 4

Ingredients:

Ingredients for the dressing

- ¼ cup blackberries

- ¼ cup extra-virgin olive oil

- Juice of 1 lemon

- 2 tablespoons minced fresh basil

- 1 teaspoon poppy seeds

- A pinch of sea salt

- For the salad

- 2 celery stalks, chopped

- 4 cooked beets, peeled and chopped

- 1 cup blackberries

- 4 cups spring mix

Directions:

1. To make the dressing, mash the blackberries in a bowl. Whisk in the oil, lemon juice, basil, poppy seeds, and sea salt.

2. To make the salad: Add the celery, beets, blackberries, and spring mix to the bowl with the dressing.

3. Combine and serve.

Nutrition:

Calories: 192

Fat: 15g

Carbohydrates: 15g

Protein: 2g

Basic Salad with Olive Oil Dressing

Preparation time: 10 minutes

Cooking time: 0 minute

Servings: 4

Ingredients:

- 1 cup coarsely chopped iceberg lettuce

- 1 cup coarsely chopped romaine lettuce

- 1 cup fresh baby spinach

- 1 large tomato, hulled and coarsely chopped

- 1 cup diced cucumber

- 2 tablespoons extra-virgin olive oil

- ¼ teaspoon of sea salt

Directions:

1. In a bowl, combine the spinach and lettuces. Add the tomato and cucumber.

2. Drizzle with oil and sprinkle with sea salt.

3. Mix and serve.

Nutrition:

Calories: 77

Fat: 4g

Carbohydrates: 3g

Protein: 1g

Spinach & Orange Salad with Oil Drizzle

Preparation time: 10 minutes

Cooking time: 0 minute

Servings: 4

Ingredients:

- 4 cups fresh baby spinach

- 1 blood orange, coarsely chopped

- ½ red onion, thinly sliced

- ½ shallot, finely chopped

- 2 tbsp. minced fennel fronds

- Juice of 1 lemon

- 1 tbsp. extra-virgin olive oil

- Pinch sea salt

Directions:

1. In a bowl, toss together the spinach, orange, red onion, shallot, and fennel fronds.

2. Add the lemon juice, oil, and sea salt.

3. Mix and serve.

Nutrition:

Calories: 79

Fat: 2g

Carbohydrates: 8g

Protein: 1g

Fruit Salad with Coconut-Lime Dressing

Preparation time: 5 minutes

Cooking time: 0 minutes

Servings: 4

Ingredients:

Ingredients for the dressing

- ¼ cup full-fat canned coconut milk

- 1 tbsp. raw honey

- Juice of ½ lime

- Pinch sea salt

- For the salad

- 2 bananas, thinly sliced

- 2 mandarin oranges, segmented

- ½ cup strawberries, thinly sliced

- ½ cup raspberries

- ½ cup blueberries

Directions:

1. To make the dressing: whisk all the dressing **Ingredients** in a bowl.

2. To make the salad: Add the salad **Ingredients** in a bowl and mix.

3. Drizzle with the dressing and serve.

Nutrition:

Calories: 141

Fat: 3g

Carbohydrates: 30g

Protein: 2g

Cranberry And Brussels Sprouts With Dressing

Preparation time: 10 minutes

Cooking time: 0 minute

Servings: 4

Ingredients:

Ingredients for the dressing

- ⅓ cup extra-virgin olive oil

- 2 tbsp. apple cider vinegar

- 1 tbsp. pure maple syrup

- Juice of 1 orange

- ½ tbsp. dried rosemary

- 1 tbsp. scallion, whites only

- Pinch sea salt

For the salad

- 1 bunch scallions, greens only, finely chopped

- 1 cup Brussels sprouts, stemmed, halved, and thinly sliced

- ½ cup fresh cranberries

- 4 cups fresh baby spinach

Directions:

1. To make the dressing: In a bowl, whisk the dressing **Ingredients**.

2. To make the salad: Add the scallions, Brussels sprouts, cranberries, and spinach to the bowl with the dressing.

3. Combine and serve.

Nutrition:

Calories: 267

Fat: 18g

Carbohydrates: 26g

Protein: 2g

Parsnip, Carrot, And Kale Salad with Dressing

Preparation time: 10 minutes

Cooking time: 0 minutes

Servings: 4

Ingredients:

Ingredients for the dressing

- ⅓ cup extra-virgin olive oil

- Juice of 1 lime

- 2 tbsp. minced fresh mint leaves

- 1 tsp. pure maple syrup

- Pinch sea salt

For the salad

- 1 bunch kale, chopped

- ½ parsnip, grated

- ½ carrot, grated

- 2 tbsp. sesame seeds

Directions:

1. To make the dressing, mix all the dressing **Ingredients** in a bowl.

2. To make the salad, add the kale to the dressing and massage the dressing into the kale for 1 minute.

3. Add the parsnip, carrot, and sesame seeds.

4. Combine and serve.

Nutrition:

Calories: 214

Fat: 2g

Carbohydrates: 12g

Protein: 2g

Tomato Toasts

Preparation time: 5 minutes

Cooking time: 5 minutes

Servings: 4

Ingredients:

- 4 slices of sprouted bread toasts

- 2 tomatoes, sliced

- 1 avocado, mashed

- 1 teaspoon olive oil

- 1 pinch of salt

- ¾ teaspoon ground black pepper

Directions:

1. Blend together the olive oil, mashed avocado, salt, and ground black pepper.

2. When the mixture is homogenous – spread it over the sprouted bread.

3. Then place the sliced tomatoes over the toasts.

4. Enjoy!

Nutrition:

Calories: 125

Fat: 11.1g

Carbohydrates: 7.0g

Protein: 1.5g

Everyday Salad

Preparation time: 10 minutes

Cooking time: 40 minutes

Servings: 6

Ingredients:

- 5 halved mushrooms

- 6 halved Cherry (Plum) Tomatoes

- 6 rinsed Lettuce Leaves

- 10 olives

- ½ chopped cucumber

- Juice from ½ Key Lime

- 1 teaspoon olive oil

- Pure Sea Salt

Directions:

1. Tear rinsed lettuce leaves into medium pieces and put them in a medium salad bowl.

2. Add mushrooms halves, chopped cucumber, olives and cherry tomato halves into the bowl. Mix well. Pour olive and Key Lime juice over salad.

3. Add pure sea salt to taste. Mix it all till it is well combined.

Nutrition:

Calories: 88

Carbohydrates: 11g

Fat: .5g

Protein: .8g

Super-Seedy Salad with Tahini Dressing

Preparation time: 10 minutes

Cooking time: 0 minutes

Servings: 1-2

Ingredients:

- 1 slice stale sourdough, torn into chunks

- 50g mixed seeds

- 1 tsp. cumin seeds

- 1 tsp. coriander seeds

- 50g baby kale

- 75g long-stemmed broccoli, blanched for a few minutes then roughly chopped

- ½ red onion, thinly sliced

- 100g cherry tomatoes, halved

- ½ a small bunch flat-leaf parsley, torn

DRESSING

- 100ml natural yogurt

- 1 tbsp. tahini

- 1 lemon, juiced

Directions:

1. Heat the oven to 200°C/fan 180°C/gas 6. Put the bread into a food processor and pulse into very rough breadcrumbs. Put into a bowl with the mixed seeds and spices, season, and spray well with oil. Tip onto a non-stick baking tray and roast for 15-20 minutes, stirring and tossing regularly, until deep golden brown.

2. Whisk together the dressing **Ingredients**, some seasoning and a splash of water in a large bowl. Tip the baby kale, broccoli, red onion, cherry tomatoes and flat-leaf parsley into the dressing, and mix well. Divide between 2 plates and top with the crispy breadcrumbs and seeds.

Nutrition:

Calories: 78

Carbohydrates: 6 g

Fat: 2g

Protein: 1.5g

Vegetable Salad

Preparation time: 10 minutes

Cooking time: 0 minutes

Servings: 1-2

Ingredients:

- 4 cups each of raw spinach and romaine lettuce

- 2 cups each of cherry tomatoes, sliced cucumber, chopped baby carrots and chopped red, orange and yellow bell pepper

- 1 cup each of chopped broccoli, sliced yellow squash, zucchini and cauliflower.

Directions:

1. Wash all these vegetables.

2. Mix in a large mixing bowl and top off with a non-fat or low-fat dressing of your choice.

Nutrition:

Calories: 48

Carbohydrates: 11g

Protein: 3g

Greek Salad

Preparation time: 10 minutes

Cooking time: 0 minutes

Servings: 1-2

Ingredients:

- 1 Romaine head, torn in bits

- 1 cucumber sliced

- 1 pint cherry tomatoes, halved

- 1 green pepper, thinly sliced

- 1 onion sliced into rings

- 1 cup kalamata olives

- 1 ½ cups feta cheese, crumbled

- For dressing combine:

- 1 cup olive oil

- 1/4 cup lemon juice

- 2 tsp. oregano

- Salt and pepper

Directions:

1. Lay Ingredients on plate.

2. Drizzle dressing over salad

Nutrition:

Calories: 107

Carbohydrates: 18g

Fat: 1.2 g

Protein: 1g

Alkaline Spring Salad

Preparation time: 10 minutes

Cooking time: 0 minutes

Servings: 1-2

Eating seasonal fruits and vegetables is a fabulous way of taking care of yourself and the environment at the same time. This alkaline-electric salad is delicious and nutritious.

Ingredients:

- 4 cups seasonal approved greens of your choice

- 1 cup cherry tomatoes

- 1/4 cup walnuts

- 1/4 cup approved herbs of your choice

- For the dressing:

- 3-4 key limes

- 1 tbsp. of homemade raw sesame

- Sea salt and cayenne pepper

Directions:

1. First, get the juice of the key limes. In a small bowl, whisk together the key lime juice with the

homemade raw sesame "tahini" butter. Add sea salt and cayenne pepper, to taste.

2. Cut the cherry tomatoes in half.

3. In a large bowl, combine the greens, cherry tomatoes , and herbs. Pour the dressing on top and "massage" with your hands.

4. Let the greens soak up the dressing. Add more sea salt, cayenne pepper, and herbs on top if you wish. Enjoy!

Nutrition:

Calories: 77

Carbohydrates: 11g

Tuna Salad

Preparation Time: 10 minutes

Cooking time: none

Servings: 3

Ingredients:

- 1 can tuna (6 oz.)
- 1/3 cup fresh cucumber, chopped
- 1/3 cup fresh tomato, chopped
- 1/3 cup avocado, chopped
- 1/3 cup celery, chopped
- 2 garlic cloves, minced
- 4 tsp. olive oil
- 2 tbsp. lime juice
- Pinch of black pepper

Directions:

1. Prepare the dressing by combining olive oil, lime juice, minced garlic and black pepper.
2. Mix the salad ingredients in a salad bowl and drizzle with the dressing.

Nutrition: Carbohydrates: 4.8 g Protein: 14.3 g Total sugars: 1.1 g Calories: 212 g

Roasted Portobello Salad

Preparation Time: 10 minutes

Cooking time: none

Servings: 4

Ingredients:

- 11/2 lb. Portobello mushrooms, stems trimmed
- 3 heads Belgian endive, sliced
- 1 small red onion, sliced
- 4 oz. blue cheese
- 8 oz. mixed salad greens
- Dressing:
- 3 tbsp. red wine vinegar
- 1 tbsp. Dijon mustard
- 2/3 cup olive oil
- Salt and pepper to taste

Directions:

1. Preheat the oven to 450F.
2. Prepare the dressing by whisking together vinegar, mustard, salt and pepper. Slowly add olive oil while whisking.
3. Cut the mushrooms and arrange them on a baking sheet, stem-side up. Coat the mushrooms with some dressing and bake for 15 minutes.

4. In a salad bowl toss the salad greens with onion, endive and cheese. Sprinkle with the dressing.

5. Add mushrooms to the salad bowl.

Nutrition: Carbohydrates: 22.3 g Protein: 14.9 g Total sugars: 2.1 g Calories: 501

Shredded Chicken Salad

Preparation Time: 5 minutes

Cooking time: 10 minutes

Servings: 6

Ingredients:

- 2 chicken breasts, boneless, skinless
- 1 head iceberg lettuce, cut into strips
- 2 bell peppers, cut into strips
- 1 fresh cucumber, quartered, sliced
- 3 scallions, sliced
- 2 tbsp. chopped peanuts
- 1 tbsp. peanut vinaigrette
- Salt to taste
- 1 cup water

Directions:

1. In a skillet simmer one cup of salted water.
2. Add the chicken breasts, cover and cook on low for 5 minutes. Remove the cover. Then remove the chicken from the skillet and shred with a fork.
3. In a salad bowl mix the vegetables with the cooled chicken, season with salt and sprinkle with peanut vinaigrette and chopped peanuts.

Nutrition: Carbohydrates: 9 g Protein: 11.6 g Total sugars: 4.2 g Calories: 117

Broccoli Salad

Preparation Time: 10 minutes

Cooking time: none

Servings: 6

Ingredients:

- 1 medium head broccoli, raw, florets only
- 1/2 cup red onion, chopped
- 12 oz. turkey bacon, chopped, fried until crisp
- 1/2 cup cherry tomatoes, halved
- ¼ cup sunflower kernels
- ¾ cup raisins
- ¾ cup mayonnaise
- 2 tbsp. white vinegar

Directions:

1. In a salad bowl combine the broccoli, tomatoes and onion.
2. Mix mayo with vinegar and sprinkle over the broccoli.
3. Add the sunflower kernels, raisins and bacon and toss well.

Nutrition: Carbohydrates: 17.3 g Protein: 11 g Total sugars: 10 g Calories: 220

Cherry Tomato Salad

Preparation Time: 10 minutes

Cooking time: none

Servings: 6

Ingredients:

- 40 cherry tomatoes, halved
- 1 cup mozzarella balls, halved
- 1 cup green olives, sliced
- 1 can (6 oz.) black olives, sliced
- 2 green onions, chopped
- 3 oz. roasted pine nuts
- Dressing:
- 1/2 cup olive oil
- 2 tbsp. red wine vinegar
- 1 tsp. dried oregano
- Salt and pepper to taste

Directions:

1. In a salad bowl, combine the tomatoes, olives and onions.
2. Prepare the dressing by combining olive oil with red wine vinegar, dried oregano, salt and pepper.
3. Sprinkle with the dressing and add the nuts.
4. Let marinate in the fridge for 1 hour.

Nutrition: Carbohydrates: 10.7 g Protein: 2.4 g Total sugars: 3.6 g

Ground Turkey Salad

Preparation Time: 10 minutes

Cooking time: 35 minutes

Servings: 6

Ingredients:

- 1 lb. lean ground turkey
- 1/2 inch ginger, minced
- 2 garlic cloves, minced
- 1 onion, chopped
- 1 tbsp. olive oil
- 1 bag lettuce leaves (for serving)
- ¼ cup fresh cilantro, chopped
- 2 tsp. coriander powder
- 1 tsp. red chili powder
- 1 tsp. turmeric powder
- Salt to taste
- 4 cups water
- Dressing:
- 2 tbsp. fat free yogurt
- 1 tbsp. sour cream, non-fat
- 1 tbsp. low fat mayonnaise
- 1 lemon, juiced
- 1 tsp. red chili flakes
- Salt and pepper to taste

Directions:

1. In a skillet sauté the garlic and ginger in olive oil for 1 minute. Add onion and season with salt. Cook for 10 minutes over medium heat.
2. Add the ground turkey and sauté for 3 more minutes. Add the spices (turmeric, red chili powder and coriander powder).
3. Add 4 cups water and cook for 30 minutes, covered.
4. Prepare the dressing by combining yogurt, sour cream, mayo, lemon juice, chili flakes, salt and pepper.
5. To serve arrange the salad leaves on serving plates and place the cooked ground turkey on them. Top with dressing.

Nutrition: Carbohydrates: 9.1 g Protein: 17.8 g Total sugars: 2.5 g Calories: 176

Asian Cucumber Salad

Preparation Time: 10 minutes

Cooking time: none

Servings: 6

Ingredients:

- 1 lb. cucumbers, sliced
- 2 scallions, sliced
- 2 tbsp. sliced pickled ginger, chopped
- ¼ cup cilantro
- 1/2 red jalapeño, chopped
- 3 tbsp. rice wine vinegar
- 1 tbsp. sesame oil
- 1 tbsp. sesame seeds

Directions:

1. In a salad bowl combine all ingredients and toss together.

Nutrition: Carbohydrates: 5.7 g Protein: 1 g Total sugars: 3.1 g Calories: 52

Cauliflower Tofu Salad

Preparation time: 10 minutes

Cooking time: 15 minutes

Servings: 4

Ingredients:

- 2 cups cauliflower florets, blended
- 1 fresh cucumber, diced
- 1/2 cup green olives, diced
- 1/3 cup red onion, diced
- 2 tbsp. toasted pine nuts
- 2 tbsp. raisins
- 1/3 cup feta, crumbled
- 1/2 cup pomegranate seeds
- 2 lemons (juiced, zest grated)
- 8 oz. tofu
- 2 tsp. oregano
- 2 garlic cloves, minced
- 1/2 tsp. red chili flakes
- 3 tbsp. olive oil
- Salt and pepper to taste

Directions:

1. Season the processed cauliflower with salt and transfer to a strainer to drain.

2. Prepare the marinade for tofu by combining 2 tbsp. lemon juice, 1.5 tbsp. olive oil, minced garlic, chili flakes, oregano, salt and pepper. Coat tofu in the marinade and set aside.
3. Preheat the oven to 450F.
4. Bake tofu on a baking sheet for 12 minutes.
5. In a salad bowl mix the remaining marinade with onions, cucumber, cauliflower, olives and raisins. Add in the remaining olive oil and grated lemon zest.
6. Top with tofu, pine nuts, and feta and pomegranate seeds.

Nutrition: Carbohydrates: 34.1 g Protein: 11.1 g Total sugars: 11.5 g Calories: 328

Scallop Caesar Salad

Preparation Time: 5 minutes

Cooking Time: 2 minutes

Servings: 2

Ingredients:

- 8 sea scallops
- 4 cups romaine lettuce
- 2 tsp. olive oil
- 3 tbsp. Caesar Salad Dressing
- 1 tsp. lemon juice
- Salt and pepper to taste

Directions:

1. In a frying pan heat olive oil and cook the scallops in one layer no longer than 2 minutes per both sides. Season with salt and pepper to taste.
2. Arrange lettuce on plates and place scallops on top.
3. Pour over the Caesar dressing and lemon juice.

Nutrition: Carbohydrates: 14 g Protein: 30.7 g Total sugars: 2.2 g Calories: 340 g

Chicken Avocado Salad

Preparation Time: 30 minutes

Cooking time: 15 minutes

Servings: 4

Ingredients:

- 1 lb. chicken breast, cooked, shredded
- 1 avocado, pitted, peeled, sliced
- 2 tomatoes, diced
- 1 cucumber, peeled, sliced
- 1 head lettuce, chopped
- 3 tbsp. olive oil
- 2 tbsp. lime juice
- 1 tbsp. cilantro, chopped
- Salt and pepper to taste

Directions:

1. In a bowl whisk together oil, lime juice, cilantro, salt, and a pinch of pepper.
2. Combine lettuce, tomatoes, cucumber in a salad bowl and toss with half of the dressing.
3. Toss chicken with the remaining dressing and combine with vegetable mixture.
4. Top with avocado.

Nutrition: Carbohydrates: 10 g Protein: 38 g Total sugars: 11.5 g Calories: 380

California Wraps

Preparation Time: 5 minutes

Cooking Time: 15 minutes

Servings: 4

Ingredients:

- 4 slices turkey breast, cooked
- 4 slices ham, cooked
- 4 lettuce leaves
- 4 slices tomato
- 4 slices avocado
- 1 tsp. lime juice
- A handful watercress leaves
- 4 tbsp. Ranch dressing, sugar free

Directions:

1. Top a lettuce leaf with turkey slice, ham slice and tomato.
2. In a bowl combine avocado and lime juice and place on top of tomatoes. Top with water cress and dressing.
3. Repeat with the remaining ingredients for 4. Topping each lettuce leaf with a turkey slice, ham slice, tomato and dressing.

Nutrition: Carbohydrates: 4 g Protein: 9 g Total sugars: 0.5 g Calories: 140

Chicken Salad in Cucumber Cups

Preparation Time: 5 minutes

Cooking Time: 15 minutes

Servings: 4

Ingredients:

- 1/2 chicken breast, skinless, boiled and shredded
- 2 long cucumbers, cut into 8 thick rounds each, scooped out (won't use in a).
- 1 tsp. ginger, minced
- 1 tsp. lime zest, grated
- 4 tsp. olive oil
- 1 tsp. sesame oil
- 1 tsp. lime juice
- Salt and pepper to taste

Directions:

1. In a bowl combine lime zest, juice, olive and sesame oils, ginger, and season with salt.
2. Toss the chicken with the dressing and fill the cucumber cups with the salad.

Nutrition: Carbohydrates: 4 g Protein: 12 g Total sugars: 0.5 g Calories: 116 g

Sunflower Seeds and Arugula Garden Salad

Preparation time: 5 minutes

Cooking time: 10 minutes

Servings: 6

Ingredients:

- ¼ tsp. black pepper
- ¼ tsp. salt
- 1 tsp. fresh thyme, chopped
- 2 tbsp. sunflower seeds, toasted
- 2 cups red grapes, halved
- 7 cups baby arugula, loosely packed
- 1 tbsp. coconut oil
- 2 tsp. honey
- 3 tbsp. red wine vinegar
- 1/2 tsp. stone-ground mustard

Directions:

1. In a small bowl, whisk together mustard, honey and vinegar. Slowly pour oil as you whisk.
2. In a large salad bowl, mix thyme, seeds, grapes and arugula.
3. Drizzle with dressing and serve.

Nutrition: Calories: 86.7g Protein: 1.6g Carbs: 13.1g Fat: 3.1g.

Supreme Caesar Salad

Preparation time: 5 minutes

Cooking time: 10 minutes

Servings: 4

Ingredients:

- ¼ cup olive oil
- ¾ cup mayonnaise
- 1 head romaine lettuce, torn into bite sized pieces
- 1 tbsp. lemon juice
- 1 tsp. Dijon mustard
- 1 tsp. Worcestershire sauce
- 3 cloves garlic, peeled and minced
- 3 cloves garlic, peeled and quartered
- 4 cups day old bread, cubed
- 5 anchovy filets, minced
- 6 tbsp. grated parmesan cheese, divided
- Ground black pepper to taste
- Salt to taste

Directions:

1. In a small bowl, whisk well lemon juice, mustard, Worcestershire sauce, 2 tbsp. parmesan cheese, anchovies, mayonnaise, and

minced garlic. Season with pepper and salt to taste. Set aside in the ref.

2. On medium fire, place a large nonstick saucepan and heat oil.

3. Sauté quartered garlic until browned around a minute or two. Remove and discard.

4. Add bread cubes in same pan, sauté until lightly browned. Season with pepper and salt. Transfer to a plate.

5. In large bowl, place lettuce and pour in dressing. Toss well to coat. Top with remaining parmesan cheese.

6. Garnish with bread cubes, serve, and enjoy.

Nutrition: Calories: 443.3g Fat: 32.1g Protein: 11.6g Carbs: 27g

Conclusion

I hope you have enjoyed these recipes as much as I have. Life with diabetes should not be hard. It is not the end—it is the beginning. With healthy dietary management, you can lead a life free from the negative effects of high (or low) blood sugar levels.

With the knowledge I have shared, you now know why you may have become diabetic, you know what this means, and now, you also know how to manage it. You are armed with resources, apps, and recipes to help you along this lifelong journey. Food is not your enemy; it's your friend.

Cook your way to health and vitality with these recipes and tips. Good things are made to share, so please help a friend find out about this way of life. Call them over for a meal, talk about diabetes, and let's help create awareness as we feast on every delectable spoonful of diabetic cooking made easy.

The warning symptoms of diabetes type 1 are the same as type 2, however, in type 1, these signs and symptoms tend to occur slowly over a period of months or years, making it harder to spot and recognize. Some of these symptoms can even occur after the disease has progressed.

Each disorder has risk factors that when found in an individual, favor the development of the disease. Diabetes is no different. Here are some of the risk factors for developing diabetes.

Having a Family History of Diabetes

Usually having a family member, especially first-degree relatives could be an indicator that you are at risk to develop diabetes. Your risk of developing diabetes is about 15% if you have one parent with diabetes while it is 75% if both your parents have diabetes.

Having Prediabetes

Being pre-diabetic means that you have higher than normal blood glucose levels. However, they are not high enough to be diagnosed as type 2 diabetes. Having pre-diabetes is a risk factor for developing type 2 diabetes as well as other conditions such as cardiac conditions. Since there are no symptoms or signs for prediabetes, it is often a latent condition that is discovered accidentally during routine investigations of blood glucose levels or when investigating other conditions.

Being Obese or Overweight

Your metabolism, fat stores and eating habits when you are overweight or above the healthy weight range contributes to abnormal metabolism pathways that put you at risk for developing diabetes type 2. There have been consistent research results of the obvious link between developing diabetes and being obese.

Having a Sedentary Lifestyle

Having a lifestyle where you are mostly physically inactive predisposes you to a lot of conditions including diabetes type 2. That is because being physically inactive causes you to develop obesity or become overweight. Moreover, you don't burn any excess sugars that you ingest which can lead you to become prediabetic and eventually diabetic.

Having Gestational Diabetes Developing gestational diabetes which is diabetes that occurred due to pregnancy (and often disappears after pregnancy) is a risk factor for developing diabetes at some point.

Ethnicity

Belonging to certain ethnic groups such as Middle Eastern, South Asian or Indian background. Studies of statistics have revealed that the prevalence of diabetes type 2 in these ethnic groups is high. If you come from any of these ethnicities, this puts you at risk of developing diabetes type 2 yourself.

Having Hypertension

Studies have shown an association between having hypertension and having an increased risk of developing diabetes. If you have hypertension, you should not leave it uncontrolled.

Extremes of Age

Diabetes can occur at any age. However, being too young or too old means your body is not in its best form and therefore, this increases the risk of developing diabetes.

That sounds scary. However, diabetes only occurs with the presence of a combination of these risk factors. Most of the risk factors can be minimized by taking action. For example, developing a more active lifestyle, taking care of your habits and attempting to lower your blood glucose sugar by restricting your sugar intake. If you start to notice you are prediabetic or getting overweight, etc., there is always something you can do to modify the situation. Recent studies show that developing healthy eating habits and following diets that are low in carbs, losing excess weight and leading an active lifestyle can help to protect you from developing diabetes, especially diabetes type 2, by minimizing the risk factors of developing the disorder.

You can also have an oral glucose tolerance test in which you will have a fasting glucose test first and then you will be given a sugary drink and then having your blood glucose tested 2 hours after that to see how your body responds to glucose meals. In healthy individuals, the blood glucose should drop again 2 hours post sugary meals due to the action of insulin.

Another indicative test is the HbA1C. This test reflects the average of your blood glucose level over the last 2 to 3 months. It is also a test to see how well you manage your diabetes.

People with diabetes type 1 require compulsory insulin shots to control their diabetes because they have no other option. People with diabetes type 2 can regulate their diabetes with healthy eating and regular physical activity although they may require some glucose-lowering medications that can be in tablet form or in the form of an injection.

All the above goes in the direction that you need to avoid a starchy diet because of its tendency to raise the blood glucose levels. Too many carbohydrates can lead to insulin sensitivity and pancreatic fatigue; as well as weight gain with all its associated risk factors for cardiovascular disease and hypertension. The solution is to lower your sugar intake, therefore, decrease your body's need for insulin and increase the burning of fat in your body.

When your body is low on sugars, it will be forced to use a subsequent molecule to burn for energy, in that case, this will be fat. The burning of fat will lead you to lose weight.

I hope you have learned something!